For the staff and supporters of The World Land Trust, Halesworth, Suffolk,
who know that natural forests of every kind are precious – N.D.

For my green-fingered dad Bruce, Grandpa Jimmy, and Pappi Rob – L.S.

HODDER CHILDREN'S BOOKS
First published in Great Britain in 2019 by Hodder and Stoughton

Text copyright © Nicola Davies, 2019
Illustrations copyright © Lorna Scobie, 2019

The moral rights of the author and illustrator have been asserted.
All rights reserved

A CIP catalogue record for this book is available from the British Library.

ISBN: 978 1 444 93819 7

1 3 5 7 9 10 8 6 4 2

Printed and bound in China

Hodder Children's Books
An imprint of Hachette Children's Group
Part of Hodder and Stoughton
Carmelite House
50 Victoria Embankment
London, EC4Y 0DZ

An Hachette UK Company
www.hachette.co.uk
www.hachettechildrens.co.uk

The WONDER of TREES

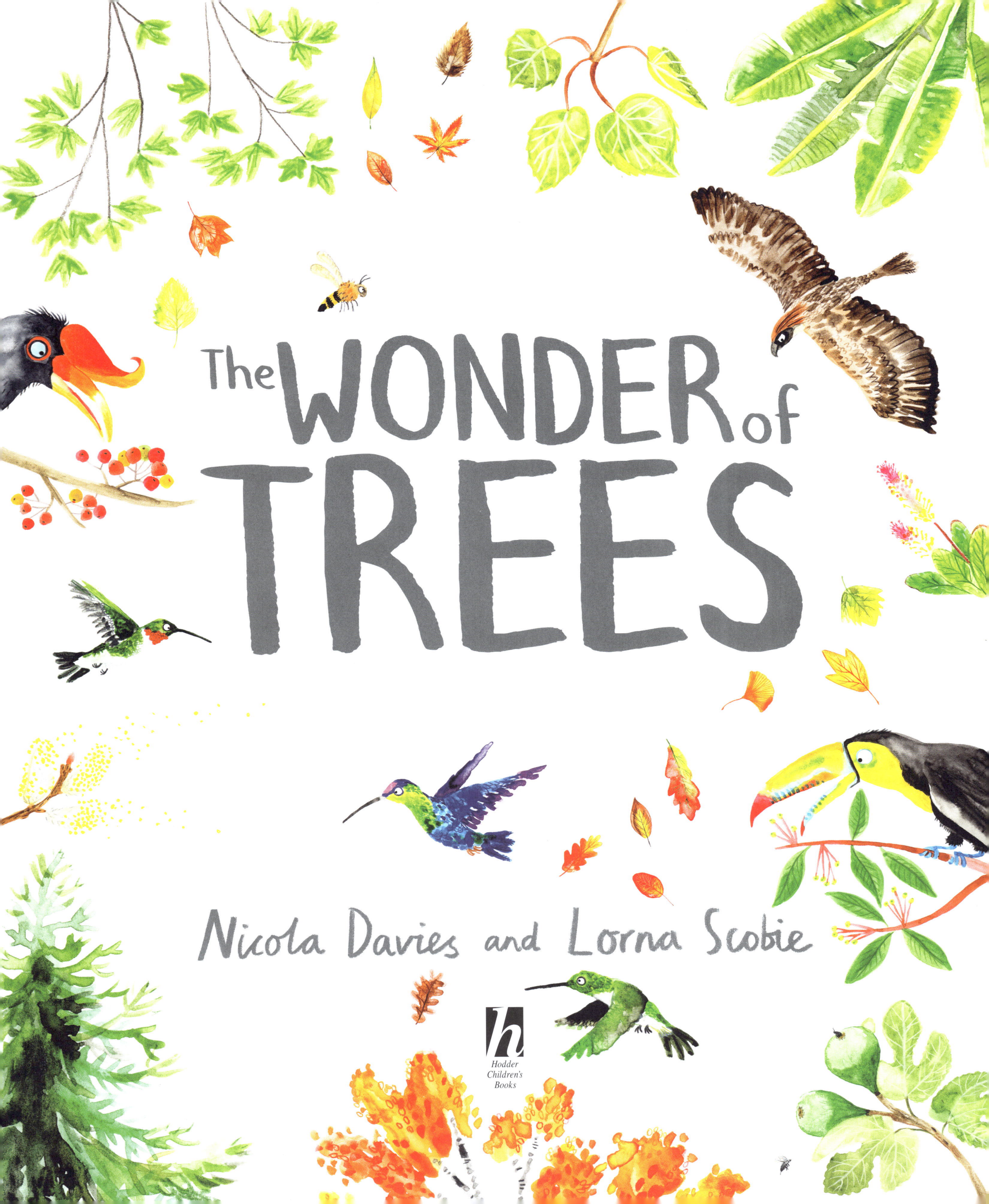

Nicola Davies and Lorna Scobie

Hodder Children's Books

INTRODUCTION

TREES ARE EVERYWHERE!

A third of our planet is covered by trees. Trees help to give us air to breathe and to create clean water to drink and to nourish our crops. They give us wood to build with, and fruit and nuts to eat.

There are two main types of trees — deciduous and evergreen. Deciduous trees lose their leaves when it's cold in winter, or when there's no rain in the dry season. Evergreen trees keep their leaves all year round.

Every tree is a world of its own, providing shelter and food to a wide range of animals, so, together, communities of trees — we call them forests — are home to a huge diversity of animal species.

Trees in towns and cities, in parks and gardens and lining our streets, help to remind us that we are a part of the natural world.

If you visited Earth from another planet and saw these huge, green beings striding across the landscape, you might think that trees ruled our world; maybe they should!

A NOTE ABOUT SCIENTIFIC NAMES

Every kind of living thing or species has a scientific name which is in two parts like this: *Eucalyptus deglupta*.

The first part tells you what the species is related to, a bit like its surname, in this case 'gum' — and the second part shows which member of the family it is — in this case 'rainbow'. No two living things have the same two-part name, so *Eucalyptus deglupta* can only mean one species, the rainbow gum.

You'll find these scientific names written after every English species name, or 'common' name, in this book.

WHAT ARE TREES?

We all know what a tree looks like: a big plant with a trunk and a crown of leaves. Plants that can grow into trees do well because they lift their leaves up into the light and shade out all the competition down below. Many different kinds of plants have found ways to grow into trees, although not all are considered true trees by scientists.

Looks Like a Tree

BANANAS have a big stem and leaves at the top, but the stem cannot last more than a couple of years. So although they look like trees, scientists would call them 'big herbs'.

DARJEELING BANANA (*Musa sikkimensis*)

WAX PALM (*Ceroxylon quindiuense*)

Almost a Tree

TREE FERNS make a trunk out of the tough stalks of their old leaves bound together with little roots. They can grow to be 15m tall and live a long time, but, to a scientist, they still aren't real trees.

Palms, not Palm Trees

PALM trunks are strengthened with wood, so they can get very tall indeed and live for a long time. But the trunk can't get thicker as the palm grows and it can't make branches, so they are called 'palms' not 'palm trees'.

SOFT TREE FERN (*Dicksonia antarctica*)

AMERICAN ASPEN (Populus tremuloides)

True Trees

The biggest and most successful trees have branches to make a spreading crown of leaves. Their trunks and branches grow thicker over time with layers of wood, to hold the weight of the foliage. These are what scientists call real trees.

BROADLEAVES have thin, flat leaves, which they may lose in winter, and catkins or flowers. They belong to the most modern group of plants, the angiosperms. Angiosperms include most kinds of plants alive today, from daisies and wheat to huge rainforest trees.

SCOTS PINE (Pinus sylvestris)

CONIFERS have narrow, spiky or needle-like leaves that they often keep year-round. They have cones instead of flowers and belong to a very ancient group of plants called the gymnosperms, which has been around for 300 million years.

Teeny True Trees

DWARF WILLOW (Salix herbacea)

Not all trees are big. The **DWARF WILLOW** gets no taller than 10cm but it is a tree, because it has a woody stem and branches that get thicker over time. It can live for over 300 years.

WHERE DO TREES GROW?

Trees will grow wherever there is enough light, rain and warmth. They grow on every continent except Antarctica and can survive everywhere, except the driest deserts, the coldest poles and the very tops of high mountains. In these places you will reach the 'treeline' — the zone beyond which it's just too tough for trees to grow.

BRISTLECONE PINE
(Pinus longaeva)

BLACK SPRUCE
(Picea mariana)

Toughest Trees

Often the trees that grow up to the treeline are conifers, as they are better at surviving drought and cold. The toughest of all is the **BRISTLECONE PINE** from the mountains of the southwestern USA. They grow slowly in harsh, dry conditions and some are over 5,000 years old.

Shaped for Snow and Sun

The tall, skinny shape of **CONIFER TREES** sheds snow easily, and makes the most of the slanting sunlight when the sun is low in the sky.

Warm and Wet

WHITE BOOYONG
(Argyrodendron trifoliolatum)

These are the conditions in which trees grow best, and where they are found, tropical rainforests flourish. Nearly all the trees in the rainforest are **BROADLEAVES**, as they can grow bigger and faster than conifers when life is easy.

BAOBAB (Adansonia grandidieri)

Hot and Dry

Trees that live in hot, dry places where the sun is high in the sky are often shaped like umbrellas to give the tree trunk shade during the hottest part of the day. **BAOBABS** are a perfect example of this type of tree.

RED MANGROVE (Rhizophora mangle)

Trees in the Desert

The **BOOJUM TREE** from Mexico's deserts has tiny, spiky branches and small leaves to help it save water and grow where there is almost no rain. It looks like a cactus, but is in fact a tree.

Trees in the Sea

MANGROVE TREES grow in airless, salty mud soaked in seawater, where other trees would die. Waxy roots keep out the salt, and stick out of the water and mud like stilts to help them breathe.

BOOJUM TREE (Fouquieria columnaris)

WHEN DID TREES BEGIN?

The first trees grew nearly 400 million years ago, when the earth was warmer than it is now and forests of trees 30m tall covered much of the land. Some of those plants have relatives that you can see in forests today.

GIANT HORSETAIL
Calamites species (now extinct)

SCALE TREE
Lepidodendron species (now extinct)

Ancient Swamp Forests

Today, **CLUB MOSSES** and **HORSETAILS** are small plants no taller than your knee, but back in the Carboniferous Period, their ancestors grew into huge trees in hot, steamy swamps. The fossilised remains of these forests are what we now call coal.

The First Conifers

The earliest relatives of conifer trees, the **CYCADS**, were munched by plant-eating dinosaurs. You can still see cycads today in some tropical forests around the world. And conifers still thrive where it is too cold or too dry for broadleaves.

SAGO PALM
(Cycas revoluta)

Modern Trees

The **ANGIOSPERMS** appeared 125 million years ago with flowers, better ways to make seeds and better ways to grow wood to make them strong. So when they began to be trees, those trees did very well. All the broadleaved species alive today belong to this big group: **THE FLOWERING PLANTS**.

AMERICAN ASPEN (Populus tremuloides)

MONKEY PUZZLE (Araucaria araucana)

GINKGO (Ginkgo biloba)

Ancient Survivors

MONKEY PUZZLE TREES have never been a puzzle for monkeys, but their spiky leaves might have given dinosaurs a prickly mouth 200 million years ago.

GINKGOES were the first trees to be able to strengthen their trunks and branches with wood. They were once found all over the world but now just one species survives in the wild in China.

Wood Trunks & Branches

Wood allows trunks and branches to grow big, strong and durable. It also helps to carry water up to the leaves, and sugary sap down to the roots. Wood is full of millions of tiny tubes, like bundles of straws. As water evaporates from the leaves at the top of the tubes, the long, thin columns of water inside pull up more water from the roots. If the tree gets too tall, these columns can snap, and that's what limits the maximum height a tree can grow to.

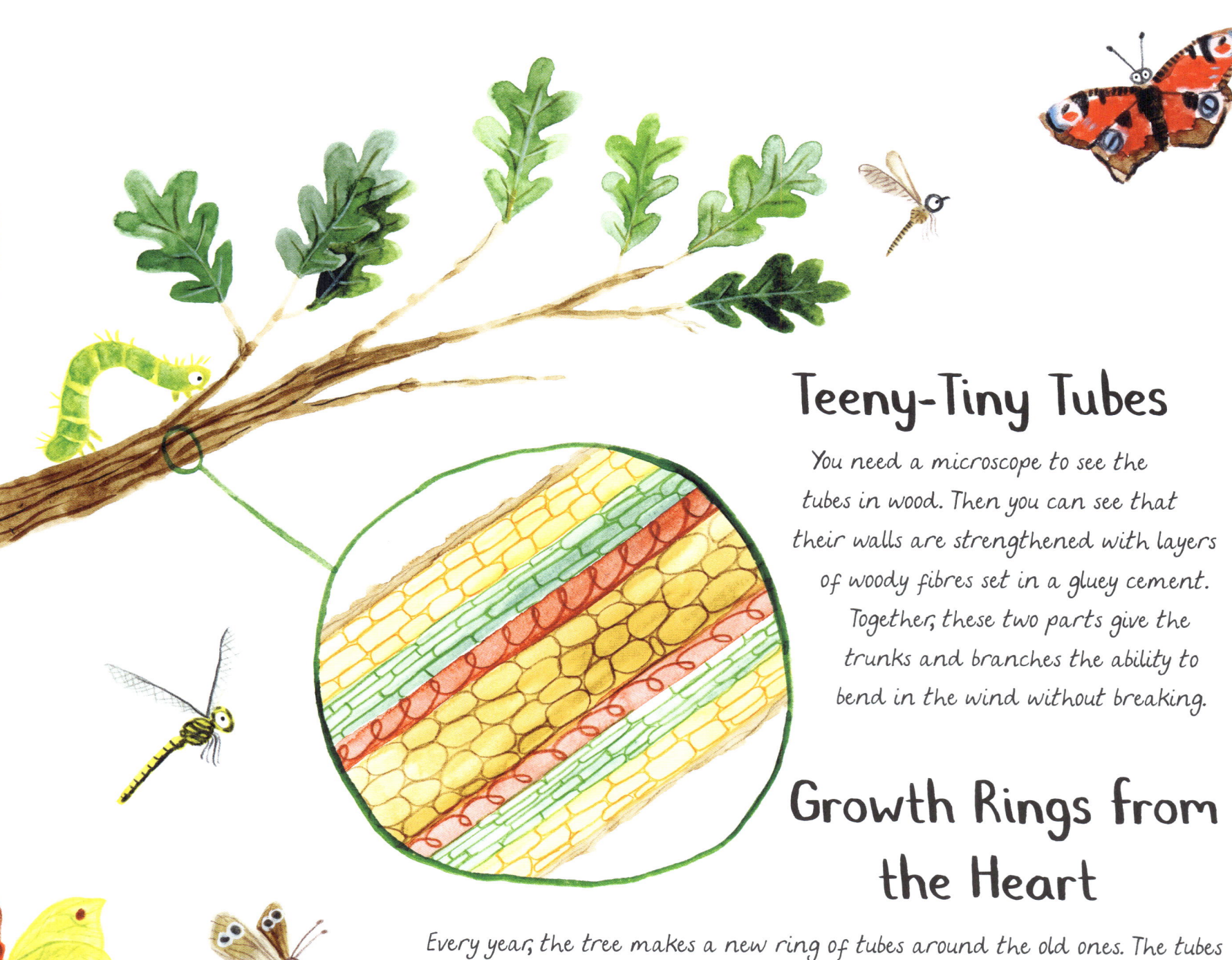

Teeny-Tiny Tubes

You need a microscope to see the tubes in wood. Then you can see that their walls are strengthened with layers of woody fibres set in a gluey cement. Together, these two parts give the trunks and branches the ability to bend in the wind without breaking.

Growth Rings from the Heart

Every year, the tree makes a new ring of tubes around the old ones. The tubes made in the spring tend to be wider than the ones created later in the year, making rings of lighter wood called sapwood. When the trunk is cut, rings of sapwood can be used to count a tree's age. In the centre, the oldest tubes become squashed and stop carrying water. They then fill with resin to form a strong, solid core, called the heartwood.

Grain and Rivets

Tubes run up and down the tree and along the branches. This creates the so-called 'grain' of the wood. To keep the branches and trunk from splitting along the grain, the tree grows woody rays that run from the newer sapwood to the old heart. These act like rivets, holding the layers of tubes together.

Wind Makes Trees Tougher

Trees in windy places grow stronger, thicker trunks and sturdier bases to their branches. Some trees even grow with a spiral grain to make them more springy and able to bend in the wind without breaking.

LEAVES

Leaves are the tree's food factories. They soak up the energy from the red and blue light in sunlight and use it to make sugar from water and air. So leaves must be in the sun, which means they risk overheating or drying out, and are exposed to rain, wind and cold. Different kinds of trees have solved these problems by having differently shaped leaves.

Evergreen Needles

CONIFER TREES can thrive where the growing season is short due to cold or drought. Their narrow, waxy leaves prevent water loss and are usually evergreen. They are tough enough to stay on the tree all year round, ready to work as soon as conditions are right.

Deciduous Cut-Outs

The cut-out edge of these **BROADLEAF DECIDUOUS TREE** leaves allows them to curl up in the wind without tearing. This helps them to cool down so they don't overheat in the sun. Most are flimsy because they only need to last a few months.

Evergreen Drip Tips

The rainforest is always warm and moist, so trees can grow all the time and keep their leaves all year round. Drip tips and a waxy surface help these leaves to shed water quickly from constant rain.

Autumn Colour

Leaves can't work when it's too cold, and winter storms can rip them to shreds. So many trees shed their leaves in autumn. But they get the most out of them first, by reabsorbing the nutrients they contain — which is why leaves turn red, yellow and then brown before they fall.

Layers of Leaves

Some trees have layers of leaves like the tiers of a big cake. Light can get through the top layers so leaves lower down can still make food. Others have a single layer of leaves that fit together like a mosaic. These trees grow more slowly and cast such dense shade that nothing can grow below them.

ROOTS

Strong, thick roots anchor the tree firmly, while tiny, hair-like growths at the roots' ends soak up water and nutrients from the soil.

Invisible Networks

The roots of a tree spread far wider than the canopy of leaves. They hold the tree to the ground and collect water for it, spreading just under the surface to catch the rain, or burrowing deep to find an underground stream.

Tree Support

Water and nutrients in rainforests are often at the surface, so tree roots aren't deep enough to keep the tree from being blown over. In this case, the tree grows above-ground roots, called buttress roots, like scaffolding to prop it up.

Toadstool Helpers

The fine, hair-like tips of roots are wrapped in a network of tiny fungal threads that reach out into the soil, collecting minerals and water. The tree swaps sugars, made by its leaves, for the water and minerals that the fungi collect. Without these fungal helpers a tree could not grow. You only know they are there when their mushrooms or toadstools appear above ground.

Talking Trees

In forests, root fungi form a huge web that connects trees together, allowing them to share food and even warn each other of danger. When a tree is attacked by leaf-eating beetles it sends a message to other trees through its root fungi, so they can toughen up their leaves, ready to resist the beetles.

BARK

Bark is the tree's skin and protects it as your skin protects you. It's made of cork, which is strong and springy and forms a honeycomb-like network of air-filled cells that resists damage, rather like bubble wrap. The outer part of bark is not alive, but underneath are living, growing cells, so if a tree is cut or loses a branch in the wind, new bark will grow to heal the wound.

COMMON OAK
(Quercus robur)

Breathing Bark

Trees need to breathe through their bark, so it has tiny breathing holes called **LENTICELS**. These are grouped together on some trees, such as the **TIBETAN CHERRY**, in raised spongy patches.

TIBETAN CHERRY
(Prunus serrula)

Rough and Smooth

BEECH TREES have smooth bark, which is hard for climbing plants and wood-eating beetles to cling to. But it takes a long time to grow, so beech trees can't heal wounds quickly.

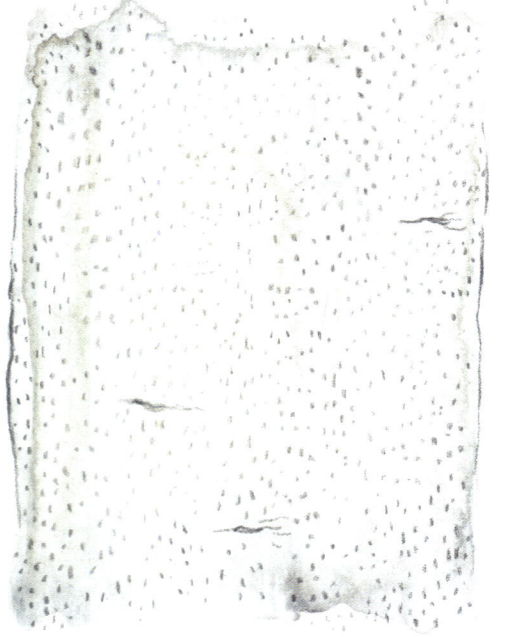

OAK TREE bark is rough and wrinkled, making it easy for insects to get a hold. But oak bark is full of bitter-tasting chemicals which insects don't like to eat.

AMERICAN BEECH
(Fagus grandifolia)

GIANT SEQUOIA (Sequoiadendron giganteum)

Fireproof Coats

Fire is a natural part of many habitats so some trees in these areas have thick, fire-resistant bark. **GIANT SEQUOIA** bark is thick and fibrous and hard to burn.

The bark of **CORK OAKS** is so thick — up to 20cm — that the heat of a fire can't get through and damage the living part of the tree.

CORK OAK (Quercus suber)

Shrugging Off Pollution

The smoke, dust and car exhaust fumes in big cities clog up the lenticels of trees. **LONDON PLANES** thrive by shrugging off their clogged-up old bark to release clean bark underneath.

LONDON PLANE (Platanus × acerifolia)

RAINBOW GUM (Eucalyptus deglupta)

RAINBOW GUM earns its name from old bark that peels off in patches to show new green bark beneath. The bark then changes colour over time.

Every tree has its own colour and pattern of bark. You can often tell what kind of tree it is, just from its bark.

PAPAYA (Carica papaya)   **PAPER BIRCH** (Betula papyrifera)   **LOBLOLLY PINE** (Pinus taeda)

FLOWERS & CONES

Just as it takes a mum and dad to make a new baby animal, it takes both male and female parts to make a seed. Trees produce flowers and cones which have male parts that make pollen, and female parts that make ovules. Pollen and ovules must come together (this is called pollination) to make a seed, but as trees can't move, they get help …

SCOTS PINE CONE
(Pinus sylvestris)

Using the Wind

CONIFER TREES have cones instead of flowers. Male cones make lots of dusty pollen that the wind blows off towards female cones.

CATKINS are the male flowers of trees such as willow, poplar or hazel. They release clouds of pollen which the wind blows to the much smaller female flowers.

COMMON HAZEL CATKIN
(Corylus avellana)

Using Animals

Many trees, especially in tropical forests, use animal helpers to pollinate their flowers. They reward them with sweet nectar and the animals leave covered in pollen that they carry to another flower.

HAWAIIAN RED HIBISCUS FLOWER
(Hibiscus kokio)

Go Red for Birds

Red is the best colour for attracting bird pollinators, like hummingbirds. Birds also like lots of sweet nectar, but as they don't have much of a sense of smell, scent isn't needed.

PEACH BLOSSOM FLOWER
(Prunus persica)

Insect Helpers

Bees are attracted to sweet-smelling flowers that reflect UV light, which insect eyes can see and ours can't.

AFRICAN BAOBAB FLOWER
(Adansonia digitata)

BAT-POLLINATED TREES have flowers that open after dark and which have a musty pong. They dangle on long stems to make it easy for bats to get their sweet reward.

FIG FLOWERS are inside the fig fruit. A tiny female wasp crawls in to lay her eggs, and when they hatch, her daughters fly to a new fig, carrying pollen. There are 700 species of fig tree and their fruit feeds birds, monkeys and apes, all thanks to a tiny wasp.

COMMON FIG FRUIT
(Ficus carica)

SEEDS

A seed is a little capsule of life. It contains the tiny beginnings of leaves and roots, plus a store of food to help the tree start growing. Trees have many different ways of giving their seeds the best chance of finding the right place to grow.

QUIPO SEEDS
(Cavanillesia platanifolia)

DIPTEROCARP SEEDS
(Dipterocarpus obtusifolius)

Carried on the Wind

Some seeds have wings that help them catch the breeze in order to be carried to a good spot. **DIPTEROCARPS** are a family of big rainforest trees from southeast Asia. Their seeds have two wings that spin like the blades on a helicopter.

Seeds of the **QUIPO TREE** are held in a papery carrier with five wings that spin in the air like a merry-go-round.

Carried by Animals

BEECH TREES don't make seeds every year, but when they do, they make so many that squirrels, mice and birds can't eat them all. They store the extra seeds for later, often burying them underground. Some are forgotten and can sprout into young trees.

Brazil nuts fall from the huge **BRAZIL NUT TREE** inside a tough, woody capsule. Only the sharp teeth of a large, rat-like creature called an agouti can break the capsule open to find the nuts. Some get eaten, some carried away, buried and then forgotten.

COMMON BEECH SEEDS
(Fagus sylvatica)

BRAZIL NUTS
(Bertholletia excelsa)

Seeds Planted in Poo!

Some trees wrap their seeds in a juicy coat. Animals and birds eat this fruit then carry the seeds in their tummy and may poo them out a long way away. Poo also provides a bit of ready-made compost to help the seeds to grow! Many rainforest trees would die out without animals to spread their seeds.

COMMON RED-STEM FIG FRUIT (Ficus variegata)

The fruits of the **COMMON RED-STEM FIG** take hours for greater short-nosed fruit bats to digest. By the time the seeds pop out, the bats have carried them miles across the forest to start life in a new place.

Orangutans eat several hundred kinds of fruits from rainforest trees and plants. Their poo spreads seeds over the forest, so they are important tree planters.

The seeds of an **AMAZONIAN RUBBER TREE** float in the flood waters that surround the trees in the rainy season. Tambaqui fish can break open and eat the tough fruits, and then release the seeds in a new place by pooing.

AMAZONIAN RUBBER TREE SEEDS (Hevea brasiliensis)

PLANTS ON TREES

It takes a lot of time and energy for a tree to lift its crown up into the light. Other plants want a place in the sun too, but without the hard work. So, some have found ways to cheat by hitching a ride on trees' branches. These cheating plants are commonest in rainforests. A single tree can hold hundreds of other plants, which add to the food and shelter a tree provides for animals of all types.

In at the Top

The first problem the cheats face is getting up into the tree. Some, like **ORCHIDS**, have tiny seeds that blow on the wind. Many also get carried by birds or other creatures. **MISTLETOE** berries contain seeds that are so sticky, birds wipe their beaks on rough bits of bark to remove them, and so plant the seeds in the perfect spot.

Tough at the Top

The only water in the treetops is rain, or mist, so full-time treetop residents, called **EPIPHYTES**, can struggle to find enough moisture. Some, like **SPANISH MOSS**, soak it up through their leaves, and can tolerate being dried out.

Others trap their own water when it rains. **BROMELIADS** have overlapping leaves that make little water tanks.

And others, like **MISTLETOES**, are parasites that steal water from the tree by growing roots into its wood.

Give and Take

EPIPHYTES cling to their perch with a tangle of roots that trap bits of dead plants, which later turn into soil. Trees benefit from these soil parcels by soaking up the goodness they contain.

Feet on the Ground, Head in the Sky

LIANAS are vines which grow from seeds on the ground. They climb up the tree trunk and then spread out in the canopy, sometimes growing through several different trees, forming important walkways for animals.

Stranglers

When an animal drops the seed of a **STRANGLER FIG** in a tree, the tree is doomed. The strangler grows down, gets its roots into the soil and its leaves into the canopy. Eventually, the tree is smothered and dies.

INSECTS IN TREES

For an insect, a single tree can be a world, and every tiny part of it a different habitat. 284 different species of insect can live on an English oak tree, and trees in a tropical forest can have perhaps ten times as many.

Many Mouths Make a Big Bite

Insects may be small but they are many! They can munch through leaves and burrow into wood, damaging or even killing a tree. So trees protect themselves with tough bark and leaves, or poisonous chemicals.

PURPLE HAIRSTREAK BUTTERFLY
(Neozephyrus quercus)

PURPLE HAIRSTREAK CATERPILLAR
(Neozephyrus quercus)

The **PURPLE HAIRSTREAK** butterfly spends most of its time flitting about in the sunlit tops of oak trees so is very hard to spot. It lays its eggs in late summer and the caterpillars hatch in spring. They hide by day and feed on new leaves and flowers by night.

GREAT OAK BEAUTY (Hypomecis roboraria)

Mottled grey wings give **GREAT OAK BEAUTY** moths perfect camouflage when they rest on tree trunks in the day. Their caterpillars feed on oak leaves and look just like twigs.

STAG BEETLE (Lucanus cervus)

The larvae of **STAG BEETLES** spend at least three years eating dead wood. They then build an underground cocoon as big as an orange, before emerging as an adult beetle.

CARDINAL CLICK BEETLE
(Ampedus cardinalis)

Every part of a tree can be home for insects. The **CARDINAL CLICK BEETLE** lives only in the rotting heartwood of old oak, ash, beech and elm trees, which makes it very hard for scientists to study.

Leaf Miners

The tiny caterpillars and larvae of small moths, beetles and wasps live inside oak leaves, eating little tunnels – called mines – sandwiched between the upper and lower surface of the leaves.

COMMON OAK
(Quercus robur)

UMBRELLA THORN ACACIA
(Vachellia tortilis)

UMBRELLA THORN ACACIA THORN
(Vachellia tortilis)

Insect Partners

Not all insects are harmful to trees. Many **ACACIA TREES** have hollow thorns for ants to live in, and make rice-like grains of food for them to eat. In return the ants sting leaf-eating animals and even cut away vines that might strangle the tree. **ELM TREES** make a scent to attract tiny wasps to kill caterpillars that are eating its leaves.

The Insects are Coming!

Trees can warn their neighbours to be ready for an insect attack by releasing warning chemicals into the air. Their neighbours get the message and put extra nasty-tasting chemicals into their leaves.

REPTILES & AMPHIBIANS IN TREES

In parts of the world where the climate is warm, reptiles and amphibians make the most of life in the treetops. A few can live on fruit and leaves but most hunt insects and other small tree-dwellers, while making sure they don't end up as dinner for something bigger.

Hunting and Hiding

LEAF-TAILED GECKOS from the forests of Madagascar have sticky toes and long claws to help them climb, and huge eyes to help them see their insect prey at night. By day they seem to disappear, blending in with leaves or bark.

CHAMELEONS are great climbers! Their feet are like pincers for grasping branches and their curly tails can cling on like an extra limb. They can change colour to match any leafy background while they track insect prey and catch it with their sticky tongues.

SATANIC LEAF-TAILED GECKO
(*Uroplatus phantasticus*)

COMMON CHAMELEON
(*Chamaeleo chamaeleon*)

Little Dragons

Tiny **DRACO LIZARDS** no bigger than a chocolate bar run around the treetops catching insects and signalling to each other with bright throat flaps. When they need to reach a neighbouring tree, they open a fan of bones and skin from their chests and glide!

BARRED FLYING DRAGON
(*Draco taeniopterus*)

SULAWESI LINED GLIDING LIZARD
(*Draco spilonotus*)

Tree Snakes

SNAKES can twine around twigs and slither along branches to catch frogs, lizards, small mammals and birds, and to steal eggs from nests. Some, known as FLYING SNAKES, can even glide from one tree to another by making their bodies into a ribbon shape, so they don't have to go along the ground to switch trees.

PARADISE TREE SNAKE (Chrysopelea paradisi)

ASIAN GREEN VINE SNAKE (Ahaetulla nasuta)

EMERALD TREE BOA (Corallus caninus)

Frogs in Trees

FROGS live in trees where there is enough rain to keep their thin skins moist. They find the water they need for their eggs and tadpoles in small pools caught in the leaves of plants, or by laying eggs in balls of froth above pools, so the tadpoles can drop into the water far below. Sticky toe-pads help them cling to leaves and branches. There can be so many tree frogs in rainforests that the night is full of their croaks and cries.

RED-BACKED POISON DART FROG (Ranitomeya reticulata)

GREY FOAM-NEST TREE FROG (Chiromantis xerampelina)

BROMELIAD TREE FROG (Bromeliohyla bromeliacia)

BIRDS & TREES

Trees give birds fruits, seeds, nectar and insects to eat, plus safe places to make their nests. But birds give a lot in return. They help to pollinate flowers, spread seeds and feed on leaf-eating caterpillars and wood-boring insects.

VILLAGE WEAVER (Ploceus cucullatus)

BLUE-THROATED HUMMINGBIRD (Lampornis clemenciae)

Treetop Homes

Many species of birds make their nests in trees where they can be safe from predators down on the ground. But there are hunters in the treetops too, so birds have ways to keep their eggs and young safe. **HUMMINGBIRDS** use spider web to bind leaves and moss into a camouflaged nest that's hard to spot. **WEAVER BIRDS** make nests like baskets with the entrance at the bottom to stop snakes slithering in.

PILEATED WOODPECKER
(Hylatomus pileatus)

Woodpecker Tree Services

WOODPECKERS have chisel-like beaks with built-in shock absorbers so they don't get a headache from pecking hard tree trunks. Their long tongues can pull out juicy insects that would damage the tree, and the holes they make for their nests may be used by other birds and animals after they have finished with them.

EURASIAN SPARROWHAWK (Accipiter nisus)

PHILIPPINE EAGLE (Pithecophaga jefferyi)

Woodland Hunters

With many animals eating leaves, bark, sap, fruits and nuts, there are plenty of opportunities for hunters like hawks, eagles and owls to locate prey arond trees.

SPOTTED OWL (Strix occidentalis)

Same Job, Different Birds

In the forests of South and Central America, **TOUCANS** use their long beaks to grab fruit from the ends of branches too thin for them to perch on. They then spread the seeds around the forest. In Asia and Africa **HORNBILLS** do a similar job.

KEEL-BILLED TOUCAN (Ramphastos sulfuratus)

RHINOCEROS HORNBILL (Buceros rhinoceros)

MAMMALS IN TREES

Trees offer safety from most big predators, but are a challenging environment. They require top-notch climbing skills and the ability to search for food in a complex, three-dimensional puzzle of branches and leaves.

Squirrelling Around

Claws for clinging and bushy tails for balance, plus strong teeth for eating nuts and sharp eyes for spotting danger, help squirrels to thrive in trees. More than a hundred different kinds can be found in forests around the world.

INDIAN GIANT SQUIRREL
(Ratufa indica)

PROBOSCIS MONKEY
(Nasalis larvatus)

GOLDEN-HEADED LION TAMARIN
(Leontopithecus chrysomelas)

Monkey Business

Monkeys come in a huge range of sizes and shapes, from the tiny **TAMARINS** of South American forests to the big-bellied **PROBOSCIS MONKEYS** of Bornean mangroves. They eat everything that trees have to offer, from sap and leaves to fruit, insects and birds' eggs.

LAR GIBBON
(Hylobates lar)

BORNEAN ORANGUTAN
(Pongo pygmaeus)

Cousins in the Forest

Apes are our closest relatives and all live in tropical forests but **ORANGUTANS** and **GIBBONS** from the jungles of southeast Asia spend the most time in trees. Orangutans have brilliant memories, so they can remember just when and where to find the hundreds of kinds of fruiting tree in their patch of the forest. Gibbons are the smallest ape, with long arms that give them the ability to swing around in the treetops, a movement which has its own word: brachiating.

RYUKYU FRUIT BAT
(Pteropus dasymallus)

The Night Shift

At night, **BATS** emerge from hollow trees or underneath leaves to feed on fruit, flowers, insects and even frogs and other bats.

PHILIPPINE FLYING LEMUR
(Cynocephalus volans)

Leapers

Big eyes and ears allow **BUSH BABIES** to find insect prey in the dark.

Tree Transport

Bats aren't the only treetop zoomers! Gliding is a quick way to get from one tree to another, so several kinds of tree dwellers can glide — squirrels and possums and creatures called **COLUGOS**.

PHILIPPINE TARSIER
(Carlito syrichta)

Big Cat Acrobat

Most predators are too big to climb around in the treetops, but the **CLOUDED LEOPARD** of southeast Asia is so good at climbing that it can hang by its back legs and move along underneath branches.

CLOUDED LEOPARD (Neofelis nebulosa)

Big Job, Small Helpers

It's hard for bigger animals like mammals to get enough nourishment from an all-leaf diet. Leaf-eating monkeys, koalas and sloths all have microbes in their gut that help digest tough leaves.

BROWN-THROATED SLOTH
(Bradypus variegatus)

COMMUNITIES OF TREES

Trees like to live with other trees, even though it means competing for a place in the sunlight and sharing water and nutrients. Living together has big benefits, so wherever trees can grow, they form communities that we call forests. Different places around the world, hot or cold, wet or dry, have different sorts of forest.

Relying on Friends

Trees in the middle of forests are sheltered in amongst other trees, so they don't need to make their trunks and branches as strong. But if they lose their neighbours in a storm, or when humans cut them down, they may not be sturdy enough to survive the winds on the forest edge.

Racing for the Light

Growing in the shade of the forest floor, young trees struggle to get enough light, but their parent trees nearby can help out by passing food through their roots. Only when an old tree dies and leaves a gap in the canopy does light reach these youngsters. Then they grow fast, racing to be the first to reach the space left by the old tree.

Food and Shelter for the Helpers

Alone, one tree could not provide enough food or shelter for the pollinating and seed-carrying animals it needs. But in a community of trees, there's nearly always something to eat and plenty of places to make a home.

Community Recycling

Over time, fallen leaves and branches make forest soil full of nutrients and friendly microbes that keep trees healthy. Old trees rot and leave nutrients that help young trees grow. Forests even help to make their own rain by breathing out water vapour that turns into clouds.

GIANT REDWOOD
(Sequoiadendron giganteum)

Mix or Match?

Most forests are a mixture of different species of tree. But **GIANT REDWOODS** cast such dense shade and grow so tall (over 100m) that nothing can catch up with them! Even their own seedlings can only grow when a big fire has destroyed some of the adults and made spaces in the canopy.

TAIGA

The taiga or boreal forest is the biggest single land habitat in the world. It is draped around the shoulders of our planet from Alaska to Siberia and the Kamchatka peninsula in Russia. Snowy winters last for eight months of the year and the temperature can drop to -50°C, more than twice as cold as the inside of a freezer. Only the toughest trees can take it.

GREAT GREY OWL
(Strix nebulosa)

WINTER

Trees

CONIFERS rule the taiga. Their needle-like leaves resist the cold and hold on to the precious water when the roots are frozen. Their dark-green colour soaks up the sun's heat fast so that they can make the most of any sunshine. But in the coldest, harshest places, keeping any kind of leaves alive in winter is impossible. Here, larches, which lose their needles in winter, take over.

Animals

GREAT GREY OWLS have thick feathers to keep them warm. Their ears can hear mice moving 60cm under the snow.

WOLVES have thick coats and tails to keep out the cold. Working together helps them survive in tough conditions.

SNOWSHOE HARES turn white in winter and have furry feet to help them walk over snow.

Small mammals like mice and voles keep cosy in tunnels under the snow.

GREY WOLF
(Canis lupus)

SNOWSHOE HARE
(Lepus americanus)

SUMMER

The short summer of the taiga zings with life. Billions of birds migrate there from further south to make the most of a feast of insects.

Mosaic Made by Fire

Summer lightning can cause fires that destroy patches of the taiga. This gives fast-growing species a chance to flourish, creating a patchwork forest with different kinds of trees.

Sleep Away the Cold

BEARS make the most of the short summers to eat and grow fat, then sleep through the winter.

Taiga Tigers

SIBERIAN TIGERS live in the boreal forest in Russia, North Korea and China. They have thick fur and roam huge areas to find enough prey, such as moose.

SIBERIAN TIGER
(Panthera tigris altaica)

Frog Lollies

Few reptiles or amphibians live where it is so cold, but **WOOD FROGS** can survive winters by being frozen solid and thawing out in the spring.

EURASIAN BROWN BEAR
(Ursus arctos arctos)

WOOD FROG
(Rana sylvatica)

TEMPERATE WOODLANDS

Where summers are long and warm and the winters not too cold, broadleaved trees do better than conifers, creating forests of oak, beech and lime with smaller plants carpeting the ground. Forests like this once covered northern Europe and much of North America before humans cut them down to grow crops. Only fragments of the real wildwood remain, like the Białowieża forest in Poland and Belarus.

RED FOX (Vulpes vulpes)

EUROPEAN BADGER (Meles meles)

Food for Everyone

Everything depends on the trees. Leaves feed caterpillars, caterpillars are eaten by small birds, and sparrowhawks eat small birds. Bark supports insect life and the birds that eat the insects. **BADGERS** and **FOXES** make their home under the roots. **WOODPECKERS** use their beaks to chisel out nest holes, find insects to eat and, in spring, to drum on trees to signal to other woodpeckers: This is my patch – keep off!

EURASIAN BLUE TIT
(Cyanistes caeruleus)

GREAT TIT
(Parus major)

Caterpillar-Munching

Small birds like **GREAT TITS** and **BLUE TITS** time their nest-making carefully. In early spring they look at the leaf buds to work out when they'll sprout and when there will be caterpillars for their young to eat.

Tender Leaves

New spring leaves are soft and tender – perfect food for caterpillars. To protect their leaves, trees add nasty-tasting chemicals to them as they grow. Caterpillars must time their hatching carefully. Too early and there will be no leaves, too late and the leaves will have grown too tough.

EUROPEAN BISON
(Bison bonasus)

WILD BOAR
(Sus scrofa)

Piggy Ploughing

WILD BOAR rooting on the woodland floor turn the soil over, clearing the ground and giving seeds a chance to grow.

EUROPEAN BISON – huge forest-dwelling cattle – were hunted to extinction more than 100 years ago. But a few survived in zoos and now have been returned to the wild in some old forests in Europe.

DRY GUM FOREST

Many places around the world have forests which can endure a hot, dry season. Almost all of Australia's forests are able to survive long droughts and fire, and to make do with unpredictable rainfall and thin soils. Their commonest trees are the gums or eucalyptus trees, which give Australian forests their unique beauty.

RED RIVER EUCALYPTUS
(Eucalyptus camaldulensis)

Gum Trees

There are almost 900 different species of **GUM TREE** native to Australia. They have long, narrow leaves that dangle down, away from the midday sun, and are tough and waxy to keep precious water in.

GOLDEN WATTLE
(Acacia pycnantha)

Plant Protection

WATTLE or **ACACIA TREES** are found in dry places across the world. Like gums, they are drought- and fire-survivors. Spines and bitter-tasting leaves keep some leaf-eaters away, and ants provide more protection in return for the hollow spines they make their homes in.

CAESIA
(Eucalyptus caesia)

Friendly Fire

Gum forests need fire. Their trees only release their seeds from hard capsules when they are scorched. They fall onto the ground, where the fire has cleared plants and killed seed-eating insects, and the soft ash is a perfect seed bed to get baby gums off to a good start.

Koalas

KOALAS specialise in eating gum leaves, but the leaves are so tough that it's hard work to digest them, and koalas get very little energy from their food. One way to cope is to sleep a lot. Koalas may spend 22 hours a day napping!

KOALA
(Phascolarctus cinereus)

Light on the Ground

Plenty of light gets between the gum leaves, so when rain does fall, these dry forests have a carpet of flowers, grass and other smaller plants, including **CYCADS** (relatives of the plants that fed the dinosaurs).

CLOUD FOREST

In the mountains of tropical countries, clouds and mist often cover the peaks, wrapping them in moisture. It is never too hot and seldom very cold. Lush forests grow, with the trunks and branches of the trees covered in plants that are watered by the clouds. Cloud forests are found across the world, but the one on this page is from Ecuador.

Plants on Trees

MOSSES, FERNS and ORCHIDS — a huge variety of plants grow on the trees in the cloud forest in great numbers, providing homes and food for many creatures.

Fog Islands

Cloud forests on mountain peaks are like islands in a sea of other kinds of habitat, and they hold species of plants and animals found nowhere else on earth.

Hummingbirds

HUMMINGBIRDS don't mind the clouds and mist, and zoom about in the treetops searching for nectar-rich flowers. Cloud-forest plants make the most of these busy pollinators and have large, bright, dangling flowers to attract them. Over 130 different kinds of hummingbird are found in Ecuador's forest.

Smaller Cats go Higher

OCELOTS and MARGAYS are two of South America's smaller wild cats. They like the mountain cloud forests where there is a variety of small prey — mice, lizards and birds. They sleep in the trees, on branches or in hollows in the tree trunks.

OCELOT
(Leopardus pardalis)

SPECTACLED BEAR
(Tremarctos ornatus)

Bears in Glasses

SPECTACLED BEARS are good at climbing and even make platforms in the trees to rest or feed on. Their strong jaws break open tough stems and nuts, and they wander widely in the cloud forest, making a meal of many of its numerous species of plants (and occasionally a few of its animals).

LINNAEUS'S
TWO-TOED SLOTH
(Choloepus didactylus)

Slow, Slow Sloths

SLOTHS are slow because their leaf diet is low in calories and hard to digest, so they save energy by doing very little. Their fur grows down from their bellies as they hang upside down all day long, and they allow green algae to grow on it to keep them hidden.

TROPICAL RAINFORESTS

Tropical rainforests grow where there is year-round sunshine and plenty of rain. They are home to more than half of all the world's species. An area the size of a sports field can hold 240 different tree species. Each region of the world has its own kind of rainforest, with species found there and nowhere else. The forests of Borneo and Sumatra, on this page, are a treasure trove of life, home to 222 species of mammal, 44 of which are found nowhere else on earth, and more than 400 species of bird.

Giants

Huge **DIPTEROCARP TREES**, more than 80m tall, dominate these forests. There are 270 different species, and 155 of them are found nowhere else on earth. Orangutans depend on dipterocarp trees for food and shelter.

Canopy Living

Most of the life in a rainforest is up in the treetops. Monkeys, birds, bats, reptiles, frogs and insects may spend their whole lives up here. There is still a lot to be discovered about the smaller animals that live in the treetops, as a single tree might be home to thousands of different species.

More of Everything

Rainforests are home to more different species of everything than any other type of forest. Borneo's rainforests contain more than 90 different species of bat!

PYGMY ELEPHANT
(Elephas maximus borneensis)

Dark Down Below

The shade cast by the rainforest canopy is dense, so not much can grow on the forest floor, but animals can move about in the shadows. **PYGMY ELEPHANTS** (just a bit smaller than other Asian elephants) make pathways running between their favourite feeding places which are also used by other animals such as **SUMATRAN RHINOS**.

SUMATRAN RHINO
(Dicerorhinus sumatrensis)

World's Biggest Flower

The strange **CORPSE LILY** eats away at the wood inside trees, then produces the world's biggest flower on the forest floor. It stinks of dead meat and is pollinated by flies.

CORPSE LILY
(Rafflesia arnoldii)

GIFTS FROM TREES

Look around your house. How many things are made of wood? Even the roof over your head may be held up by wooden beams. From the ship that Columbus sailed in, to the piano Beethoven composed on, wood has been a huge part of human history. But even today, when so much is made of plastic, there are other vital things trees give us: water to drink and air to breathe.

Every Breath You Take

As trees use sunlight to make food — the process known as photosynthesis — they breathe out oxygen, which is just what animals need to breathe in. A quarter of the oxygen that you breathe comes from trees.

Weather Calming

Forests help to prevent floods and droughts. They act like giant sponges soaking up rain as it falls and slowing down the flow of water to streams and rivers, so they don't fill too quickly and burst their banks.

The shade of trees cools the ground, so water evaporates more slowly and soil doesn't get too dry. This prevents the formation of deserts.

Rivers in the Sky

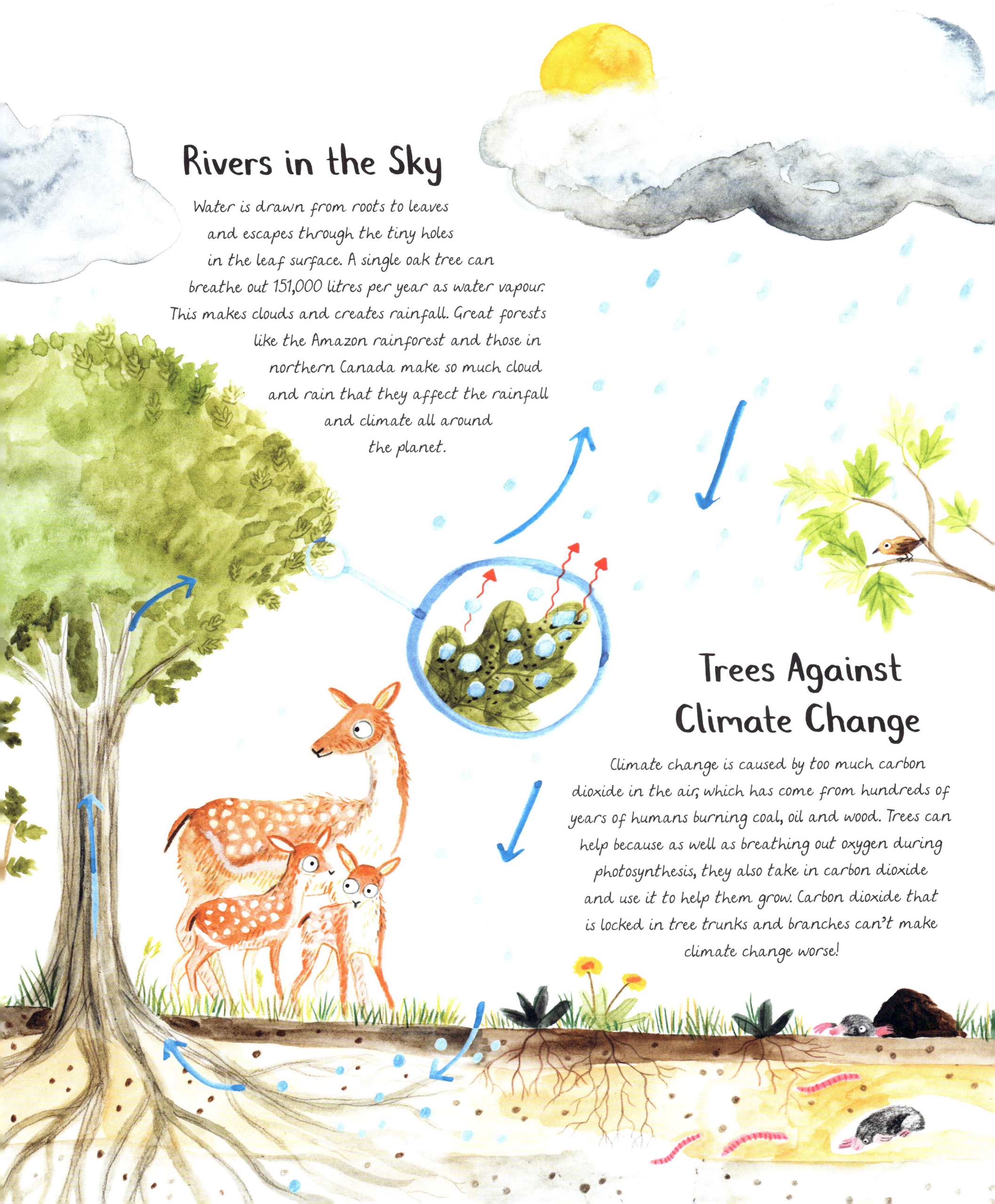

Water is drawn from roots to leaves and escapes through the tiny holes in the leaf surface. A single oak tree can breathe out 151,000 litres per year as water vapour. This makes clouds and creates rainfall. Great forests like the Amazon rainforest and those in northern Canada make so much cloud and rain that they affect the rainfall and climate all around the planet.

Trees Against Climate Change

Climate change is caused by too much carbon dioxide in the air, which has come from hundreds of years of humans burning coal, oil and wood. Trees can help because as well as breathing out oxygen during photosynthesis, they also take in carbon dioxide and use it to help them grow. Carbon dioxide that is locked in tree trunks and branches can't make climate change worse!

PEOPLE OF THE FOREST

Much of the forest that covered most of Europe and North America was cut down hundreds or even thousands of years ago to make way for farms, cities and roads. Now, the rainforests of the Amazon, Asia and Africa face the same fate. But there are people who have always lived in these forests, whose lives show us how to live in harmony with trees and protect forests.

Spiders for Dinner

To survive in a rainforest, humans must know every plant and animal, and be prepared to eat anything that will give nourishment. For the **PIAROA** people of the forests of Venezuela that means eating giant tarantulas, and it is the job of children to catch them!

Highest Treehouse in the World

The **KOROWAI** people from West Papau, in Indonesia, build treehouses high above the forest floor, big enough for a whole family to live in. They hunt huge cassowary birds and catch fish using bows and arrows, eat wild fruits and grow vegetables in gardens between the trees. On special occasions, they feast on fat sago grubs – the larvae of beetles.

Tiger Guardians

The **SOLIGA** people depend on the wild forests of the Western Ghats in southern India for food and materials to build their shelters. The Soliga believe every part of the forest is holy, especially its tigers. Numbers of endangered tigers have increased where Soliga people are allowed to live in nature reserves alongside the animals.

Tree Music

For thousands of years the **BAKA** people from the Central African rainforest have used bird-like calls to communicate through the dense green of the forest. These calls have become part of their music, and Baka musicians now travel to share their stories to help Baka people stick together and protect their forest from miners and loggers who would destroy it.

Forest Medicine

Native people from Southeast Asian forests use 6,500 different kinds of plants as medicine, and the people of the Amazon over 1,300. It's important that this traditional knowledge is preserved as a precious resource that could produce new treatments in the future. Forests, and the people who know them best, need protection!

FOREST DESTRUCTION

When humans had to use axes and saws it took a long time to fell a single tree. But now we have giant machines that can destroy a tree in seconds and we are cutting down forests fast. Between 1990 and 2015 the earth lost 129 million hectares of forest — that's equivalent to the whole of South Africa — and every five days we lose an area of rainforest the size of London.

Why Destroy Forests?

The short answer is 'to make money'. Forests are cut down so the trees can be sold for wood or to make room for cattle-ranching or mining. But the money that these activities make is less than the long-term value of what the forest provides — clean air and water, protection for the world's climate and the unknown potential of the many species that live there.

Breaking Up Forests

You don't have to cut down a forest to destroy it. A forest is a web of connections between trees and animals that all depend on each other. Take away the animals and the trees may not be able to make or spread their seeds. Take away just some of the trees and the animals may die. Break up a forest with a big road and vital connections between trees and animals may be cut.

Healing and Replanting

Every forest is a complex community of plants and animals, so it's very hard for it to regrow once destroyed. Tropical forests often grow where there is almost no soil. Without trees, the ground bakes as hard as concrete and nothing will grow. But patches of forest can be replanted and healed if there is some unharmed forest nearby.

Fight for Forests

The first step to saving forests is knowing how important they are and telling other people about it (so you can start doing that right now!). The next is to help conservation charities that are working to protect forests around the world. You might also be able to create your own mini forest in your school, community or back garden. Even one tree will support wildlife and do a little bit to help fight climate change.

How to Plant a Tree

It takes work to plant a tree: digging a hole for its roots, watering it as it grows and being very patient! But a tree will repay all the effort you put in. While it is small you can watch it grow and change with the seasons; as it gets bigger you will see creatures making it their home and you will know that far into the future it will continue to provide food and shelter for animals and pleasure for people.

Tips for Tree Planting

Choose a tree that is native to the country where you live (don't try growing a tropical tree where you get six feet of snow every winter).

1. If you live in a city, choose a tree that will survive pollution from cars.

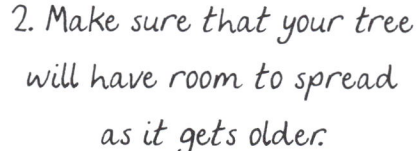

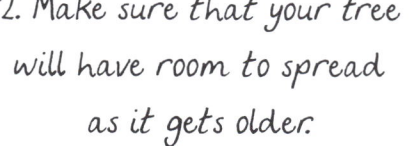

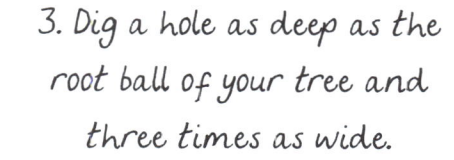

2. Make sure that your tree will have room to spread as it gets older.

3. Dig a hole as deep as the root ball of your tree and three times as wide.

4. Put your tree in, and make sure it's upright. Refill the hole, making sure soil goes right round the roots, and press down firmly.

5. Drive a stake into the soil next to your tree and tie it loosely to the trunk, so your tree has a bit of support when it starts to grow.

6. Water it and add a layer of mulch around the trunk.

City Trees

You don't have to live in the countryside to plant a tree. Parks, gardens, the side of roads — all of these places need trees. Trees in cities can have a big effect, cooling down hot sun-baked pavements, improving air quality and cheering people up by offering them the calming touch of nature.

Start a Community Orchard

Is there an area of ground in your town that no one uses? How about asking if you and your friends can plant it with fruit trees for everyone — including the birds and bees — to enjoy?

Other Ways to Help Trees and Forests

There are several conservation charities that offer donation programmes so you can save the rainforest an acre at a time. If you don't have a place to plant trees, try this: measure your school yard, or the park nearby, or even the car park of the supermarket. Then run fundraising events (cake stalls, sponsored swims and so on) to raise enough money to plant or save an area of rainforest the same as the area you measured.

Never forget, people need trees!

GLOSSARY

ALGAE
Seaweeds and tiny plant microbes that grow on larger plants or float in oceans and lakes are called algae. They are some of the simplest plants on earth but some of the most important, as the ones in the ocean make most of the oxygen in the air we breathe.

AMPHIBIAN
Amphibians, like frogs, toads and newts, breathe through their thin, wet skin and must stay moist to survive. They lay eggs, usually in fresh water, which hatch into legless 'tadpoles', before growing legs, and changing into adult form.

CACTUS
A desert plant with thick, fleshy stems or leaves that store water, and a waxy skin and sharp spines to protect that precious store of moisture. Cactuses are found only on the American continents. Plants that look like cactuses in Africa actually belong to the Euphorbia plant family.

CONSERVATION
Protecting plants, animals and the places they live from damage and destruction caused by human activities.

DECIDUOUS
Trees which lose their leaves in autumn or at the start of the dry season and grow new ones in spring or in the rainy season.

EVERGREEN

Trees which keep their leaves all year round, such as many conifers and tropical rainforest trees. Evergreen leaves are stronger and tougher than deciduous leaves, and are made to last for several years.

FUNGUS

Fungi (the plural of fungus) are living things that can't make their own food from sunlight, as plants do, or eat other living things, as animals do. Instead they live by digesting dead material, in a process often called 'rotting'. They can be microscopic, for example the yeast that makes bread rise, or large, like the fungi that break down dead trees. Animals could not live without plants, and plants could not live without fungi. Over 75,000 species of fungus are known.

INSECT

Insects' bodies have a tough, armour-like covering called an exoskeleton. They have three pairs of bendable, jointed legs, and a body divided into three parts: head, thorax and abdomen. They usually have two pairs of wings. Beetles, bees and butterflies are all kinds of insect.

LARVA (Plural larvae)

A larva is the young form of an animal that is very different to the adult form. For example, a caterpillar is the larva of a butterfly and a tadpole is the larva of a frog.

GLOSSARY

LENTICEL
A lenticel is an area on the trunk of a tree where tiny holes allow gases in and out. The area around these holes is often rough, unlike the smooth bark which surrounds them.

MAMMAL
Mammals breathe air through lungs, are warm-blooded (which means they can keep their bodies at a steady warm temperature) and have fur or hair. Females give birth to live young (except for spiny anteaters and the duck-billed platypus, which lay eggs) and feed their babies on milk produced by mammary glands.

MICROBE
A microbe is a living thing that is too small to see with the naked eye. Bacteria, viruses and some fungi are all forms of microbe. Some cause diseases but others are important parts of the natural world, helping to break down dead plants and animals to recycle the nutrients in their bodies.

MIGRATE
Animals that move from one location to another in a seasonal pattern are said to migrate. For example, European swallows migrate from Africa to Europe in the spring and back again in the autumn.

MINERAL
A chemical compound found in soil or rocks. Both animals and plants need certain minerals to grow and stay healthy. Plants get minerals from the soil through roots, and animals get them from the food they eat.

NECTAR
The sweet, sugary liquid that flowers make to tempt insects, birds and other creatures to visit them. The flower can then dust the creatures with pollen to carry to another flower.

OVULE
The word 'ovule' means 'little egg'. It is the female part of a plant that will grow into a seed, but only when it is fertilised by pollen from the male part.

PARASITE
A plant or animal that uses the body of another living thing as a place to live. Fleas, head lice and mistletoe plants are all parasites.

PHOTOSYNTHESIS
Plants soak up the energy from sunlight, using a pigment called chlorophyll which gives leaves their green colour. They use this energy to make sugar from water and carbon dioxide from the air. This process is called 'photosynthesis' and without it there would be no life on earth.

GLOSSARY

POLLEN/POLLINATION
Pollination is when pollen, a fine powder produced by the male parts of the plant, reaches the female parts, or ovules. Pollen can be carried by the wind, or by animals — such as bees or hummingbirds.

PREDATOR
An animal that lives by hunting, killing and eating other animals.

PREY
Prey animals are the food of predators. Any animal that is regularly hunted and killed by a predator is a prey animal. For example, gazelle are the prey of cheetahs, giant squid are the prey of sperm whales, and caterpillars are the prey of blue tits.

REPTILE
Reptiles breathe through lungs, have a tough, scaly skin and are cold-blooded (which means they can't keep warmer or cooler than their environment). Most lay leathery eggs, but some hatch their eggs inside their bodies and give birth to live young.

RESIN
A thick, sticky liquid produced by some plants, such as conifers. It oozes out if any part of the plant is cut, and helps to seal the wound and protect the plant from germs and insects.

SAP

The watery contents of plants. Sap acts like blood and carries food and nutrients around the plant, but also helps to keep the shape of leaves and green stems, by plumping them up, like the air in an airbed.

SEEDLING

Plants have many ways of making new plants. These can sprout from roots or even branches. Gardeners can also make new plants by taking 'cuttings' — small sections of roots or shoots — and planting them in pots. But a seedling is a young plant that has grown straight from a seed.

SPECIES (pronounced SPEE-SEES or SPEE-SHEES)

A kind of living thing. Each species of animal, plant or fungus has features which help it to survive and make it different from every other species, for example, one tree species may have spiny leaves to keep hungry mouths at bay, whilst another may have waxy leaves to shed rainwater. Living things can usually only breed with other members of their species.

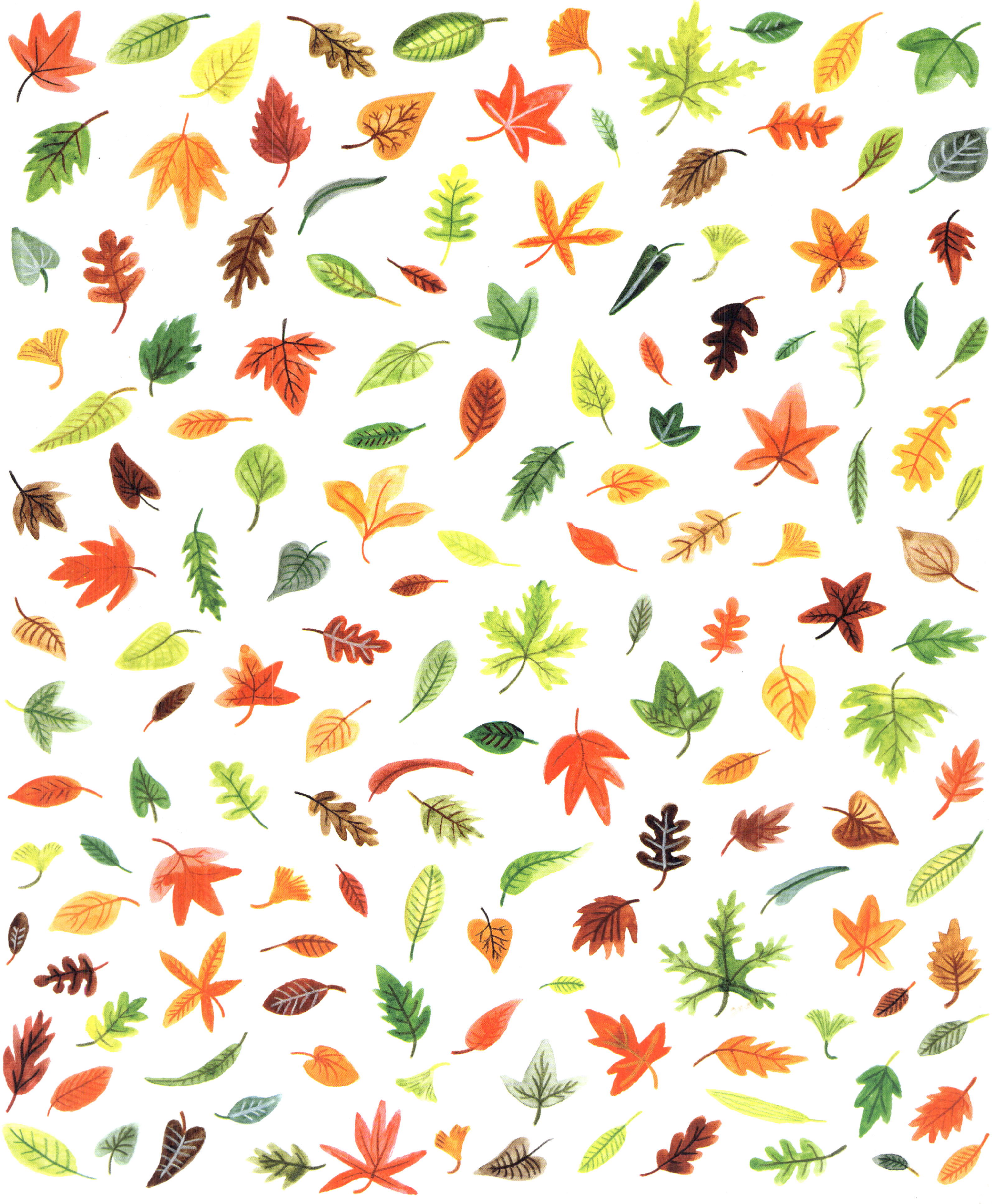